The Montessori Method

NUMBERS

A Preschool Activity Book

Text by Chiara Piroddi
Illustrations by Agnese Baruzzi

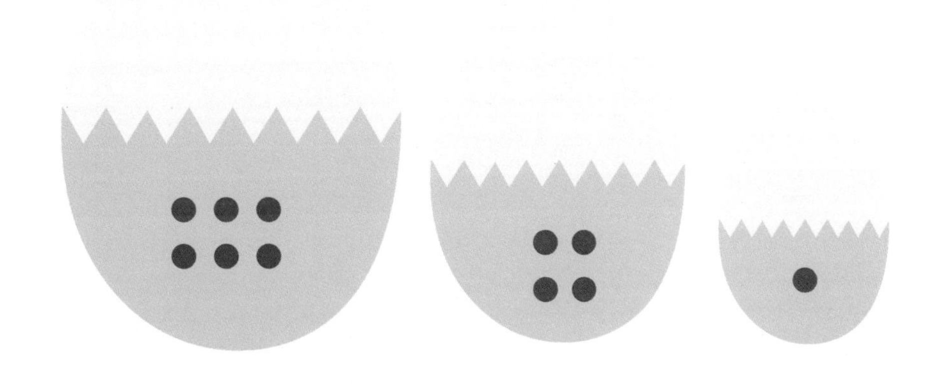

STERLING CHILDREN'S BOOKS
New York

THE MONTESSORI METHOD: NUMBERS

Creativity, freedom of choice, simplicity, variety, and enjoyment are the hallmarks of a Montessori education. These are the elements we've brought together to create *The Montessori Method: Numbers*. This activity book, aimed at children ages 4 to 6, uses fun games and strategy-orientated activities to strengthen your child's cognitive development through play.

While the activities in the book become increasingly complex as the book progresses, allow your child to begin with whatever page seems most appealing! Once you've read the simple instructions for each activity, sit back and let your child to work at his or her own pace. The book is meant to inspire independence and exploration. Encourage your child to play games, color drawings, experiment with finger painting, position stickers, or cut out adorable animals to be saved for future games.

It is important not to interrupt your child explorer while he or she is concentrated on carrying out each activity. Try not to intervene to correct mistakes, because the exercises are structured to help young learners become aware of their own errors and learn to self-correct. If some of the activities seem too complex, just encourage your child to try them again later.

The structure of the activities falls in line with the three Montessorian progressive stages of learning:

1. Presentation

This is when the child is introduced to a concept (a new number, for example).

2. Recognition

Here, the child is allowed to further develop understanding through games, activities, and various experiences that reinforce the new concept. In this book, for example, your child will learn to identify each number by name, then to determine each number's value, then to read and write the numbers.

3. Recall

In the final stage of learning, the child is able to answer questions about the concept to demonstrate mastery.

The activities in this book follow these stages of learning. This book will:

- Present the numbers 0 through 9, associating them with groups of objects from everyday life
- Encourage your child to recognize and explore the numbers through hands-on activities that build motor skills, such as coloring and cutting out figures
- Ask your child to recall numbers through simple testing activities, like using stickers to complete pictures

The symbols at the top right corner of each page indicate the materials your child will need to complete the activity.

This is what each symbol means:

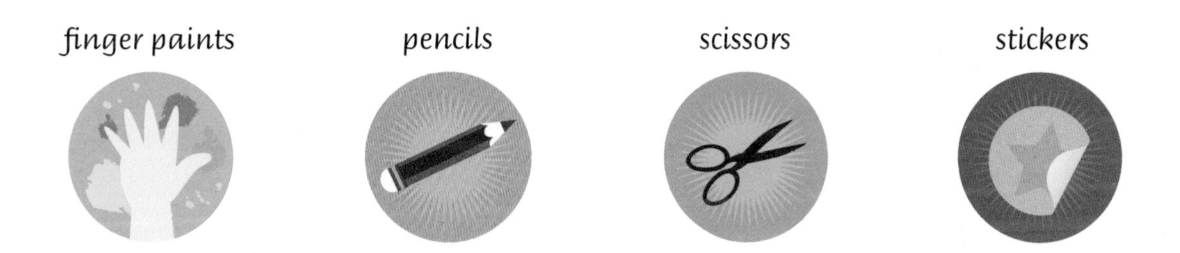

The Pedagogy of Maria Montessori

Maria Montessori was an enlightened teacher, who, at the start of the 20th century revolutionized the way we think about child development and education. Her writings focus on the true nature of the child. In her view, children are explorers, blessed from an early age with profound cognitive richness, which, with the right stimuli and encouragement, grows into knowledge. In Montessorian pedagogy, knowledge develops through the senses, so tactile, auditory, and visual experiences are essential. Learning is nourished by freedom of choice, practical experience, and direct experimentation.

Helping a child to grow means encouraging spontaneous play, respecting gradual discovery, and tolerating mistakes so that a child can develop the satisfaction of learning independently at his or her own pace.

THE NUMBERS XYLOPHONE

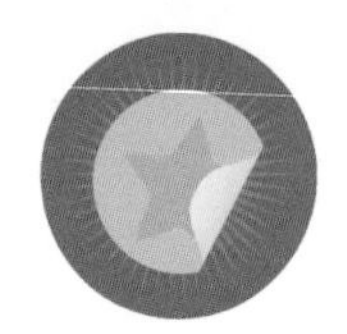

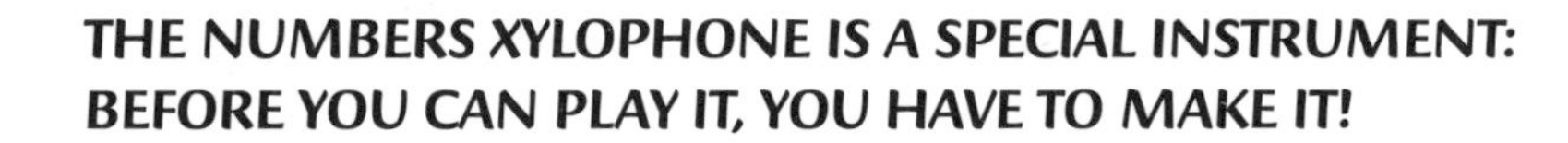

THE NUMBERS XYLOPHONE IS A SPECIAL INSTRUMENT: BEFORE YOU CAN PLAY IT, YOU HAVE TO MAKE IT!

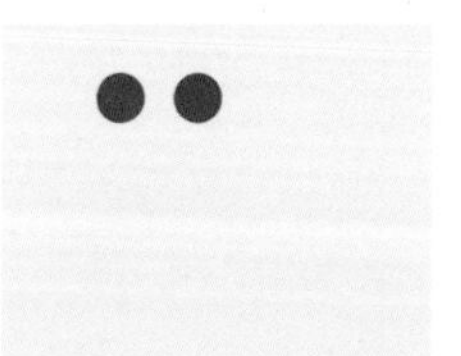

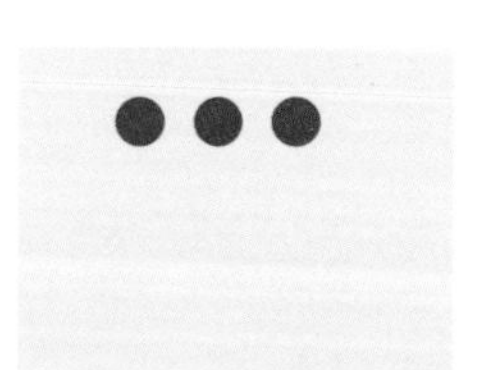

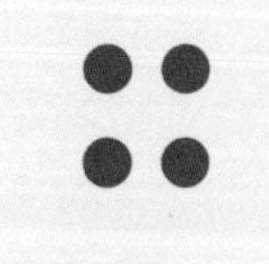

Find the stickers that go with THE NUMBERS XYLOPHONE at the back of the book.

Place the stickers in the right order.

Use the quantities, shapes, and colors to help.

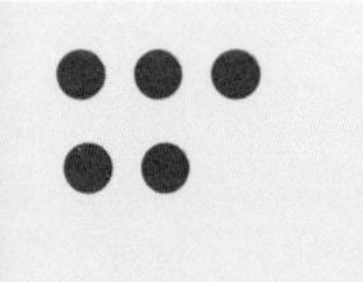

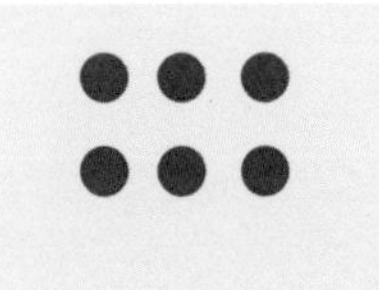

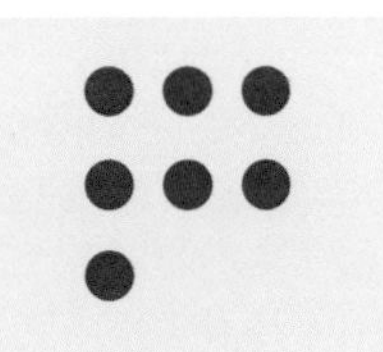

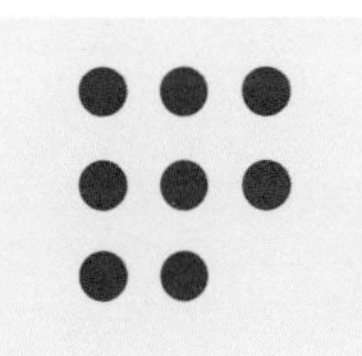

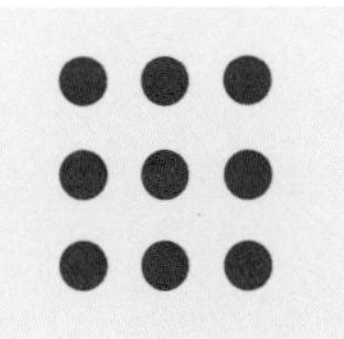

Catch the Numbers

LOOK FOR ALL THE NUMBERS HIDDEN IN THE PAGE AND CATCH THEM BY DRAWING A CIRCLE AROUND EACH ONE.

THE VALUE OF NUMBERS

Color each card with 1 object blue.
Color each card with 2 objects red.
Color each card with 3 objects green.

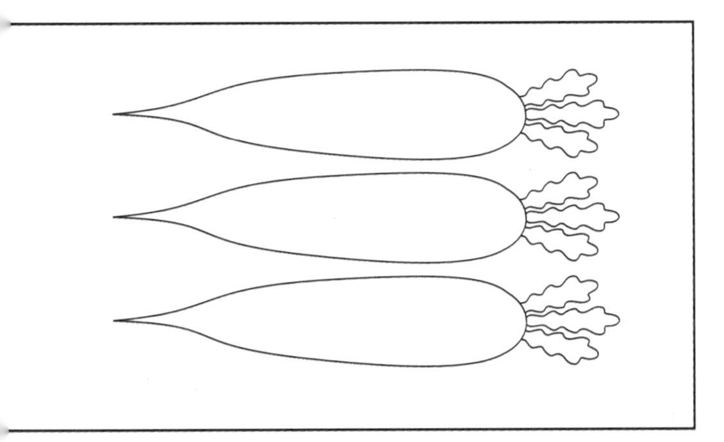

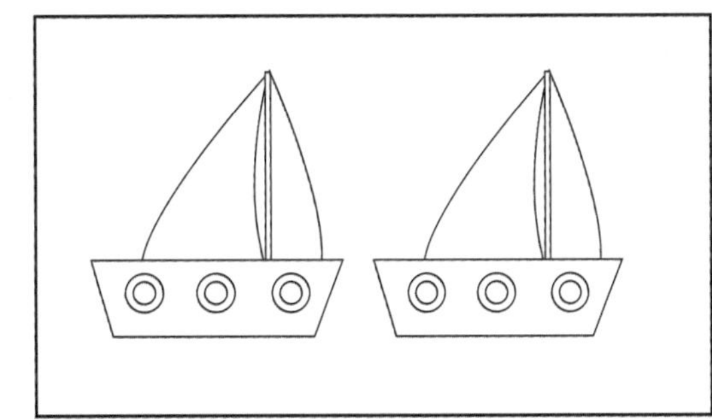

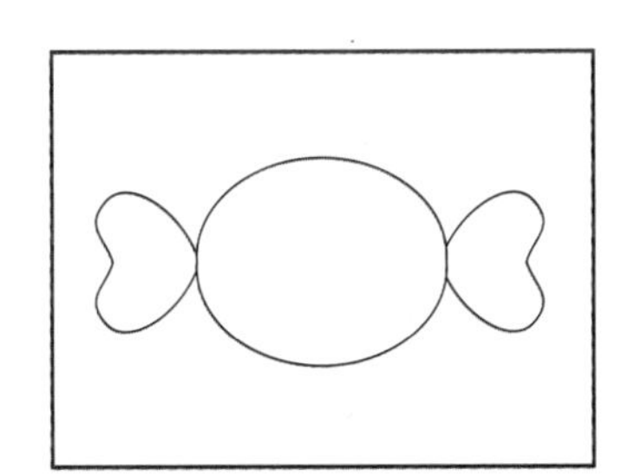

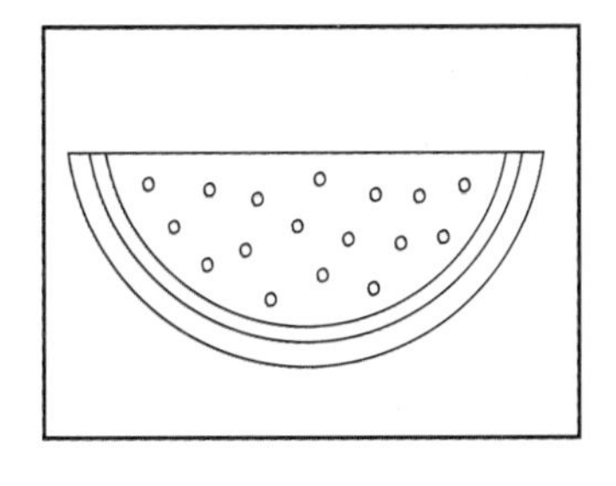

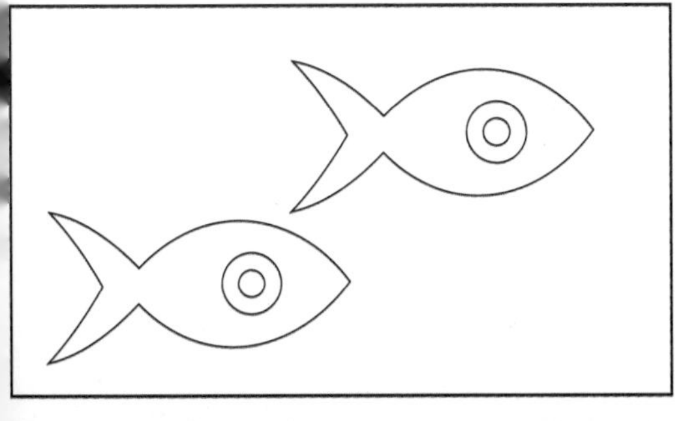

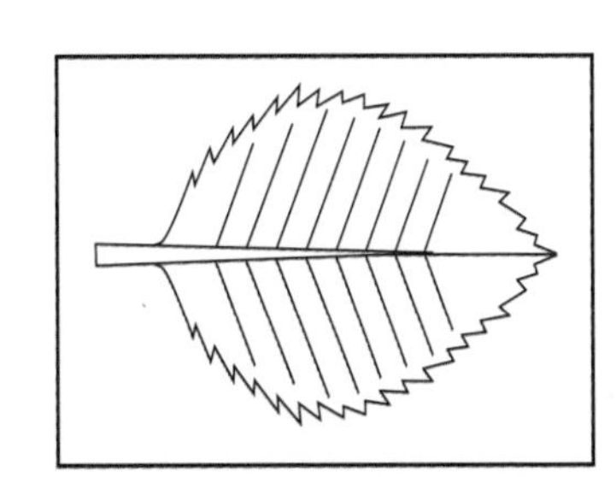

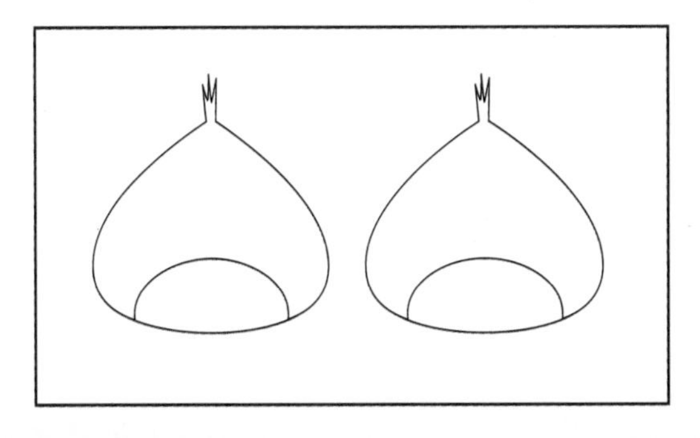

TRAFFIC AT THE AIRPORT

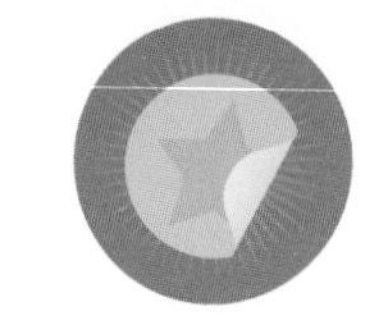

AT THE AIRPORT THE RUNWAYS ARE FULL OF PLANES READY TO TAKE OFF! LINE THEM UP AND GET THEM READY TO DEPART.

Find the stickers that go with TRAFFIC AT THE AIRPORT *at the back of the book.*

Count the number of spaces on each runway.

Place that number of stickers on each runway.

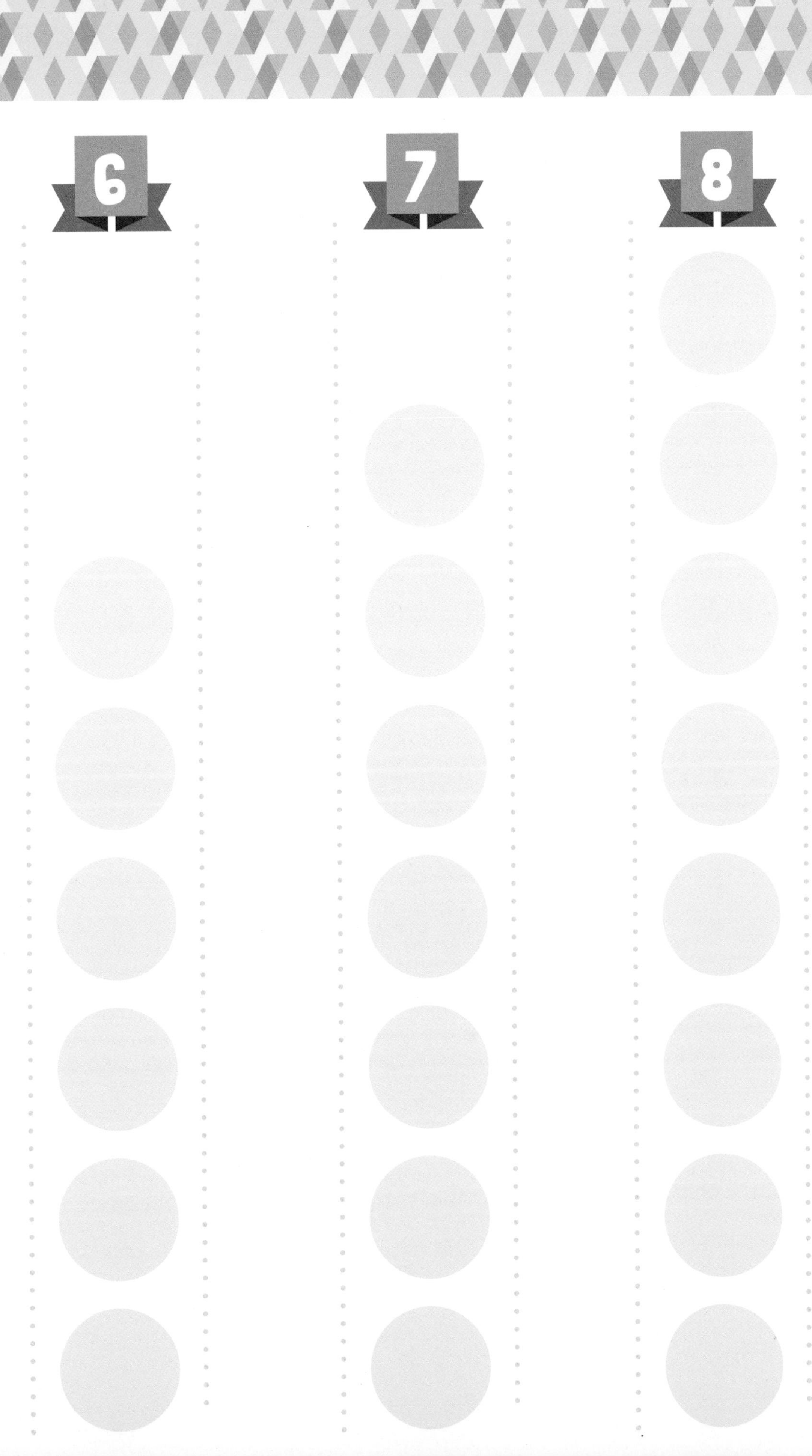
6
7
8

THE PETALS FLY AWAY

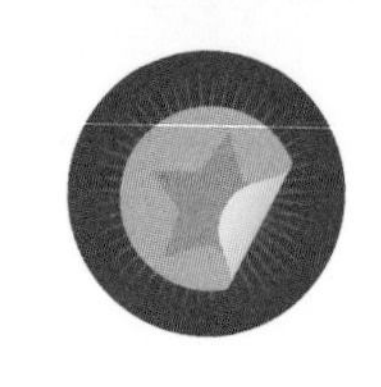

THE NORTHERN WIND BLOWS WILDLY, STRIPPING THE FLOWERS OF THEIR PETALS.

Find the stickers that go with THE PETALS FLY AWAY *at the back of the book.*

Look at the drawing and count how many petals are left on each flower.

Place that number of stickers on each flower.

Taco's acorns

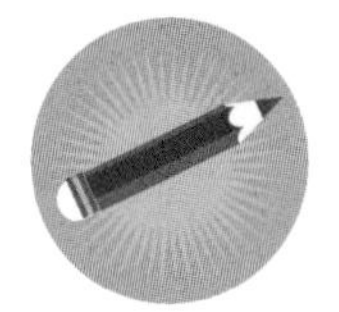

**LITTLE TACO IS STORING ACORNS FOR THE WINTER.
HELP HIM COLLECT THEM ALL.**

Circle all the acorns you find along the path.

Count them.

Color the number that matches the number of acorns you collected.

ALFRED'S APPLES

IN GRANDPA ALFRED'S GARDEN THE APPLES ARE RIPE. HOW MANY ARE THERE?

Color the apples.

Count them one by one.

Connect the dots from red to blue on the number that matches how many apples you collected.

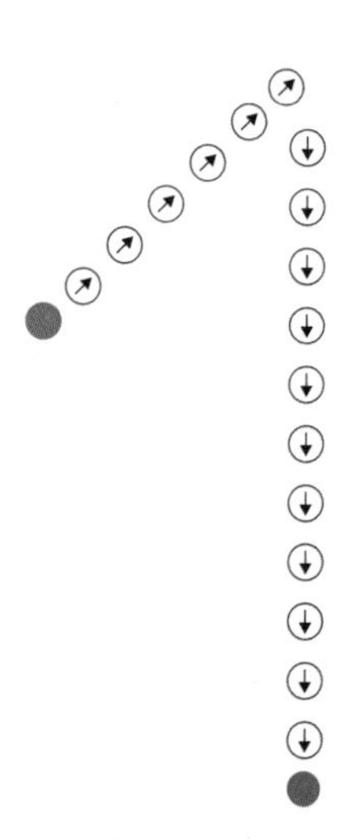

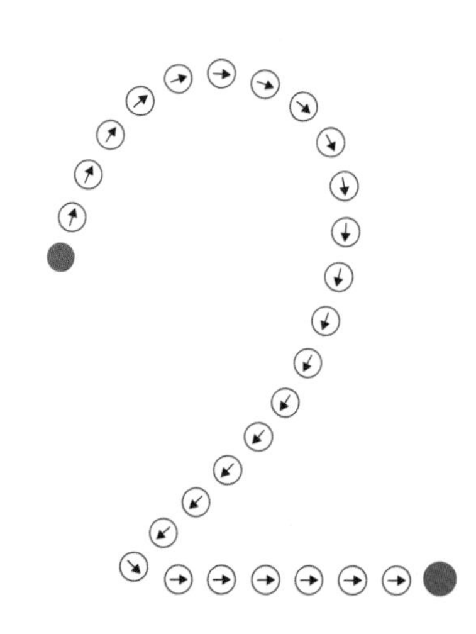

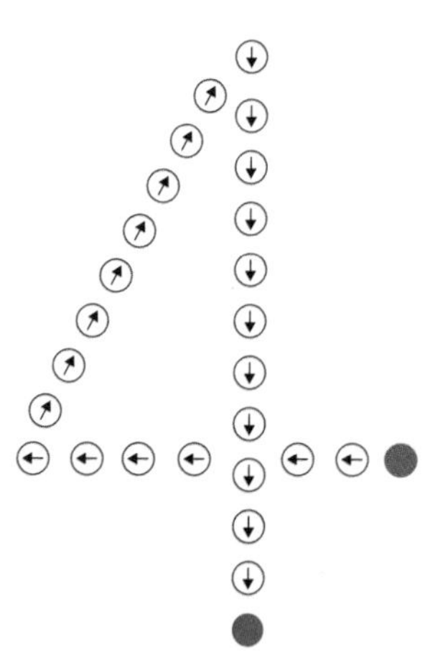

The Ostrich Eggs

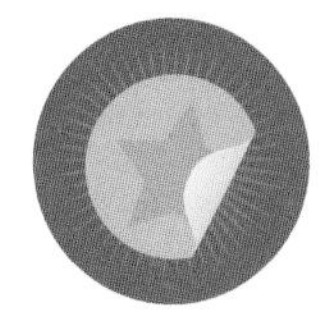

Find the stickers that go with THE OSTRICH EGGS at the back of the book.

Place the correct sticker on top of each egg bottom.

Use the number of dots and size of the eggs to help.

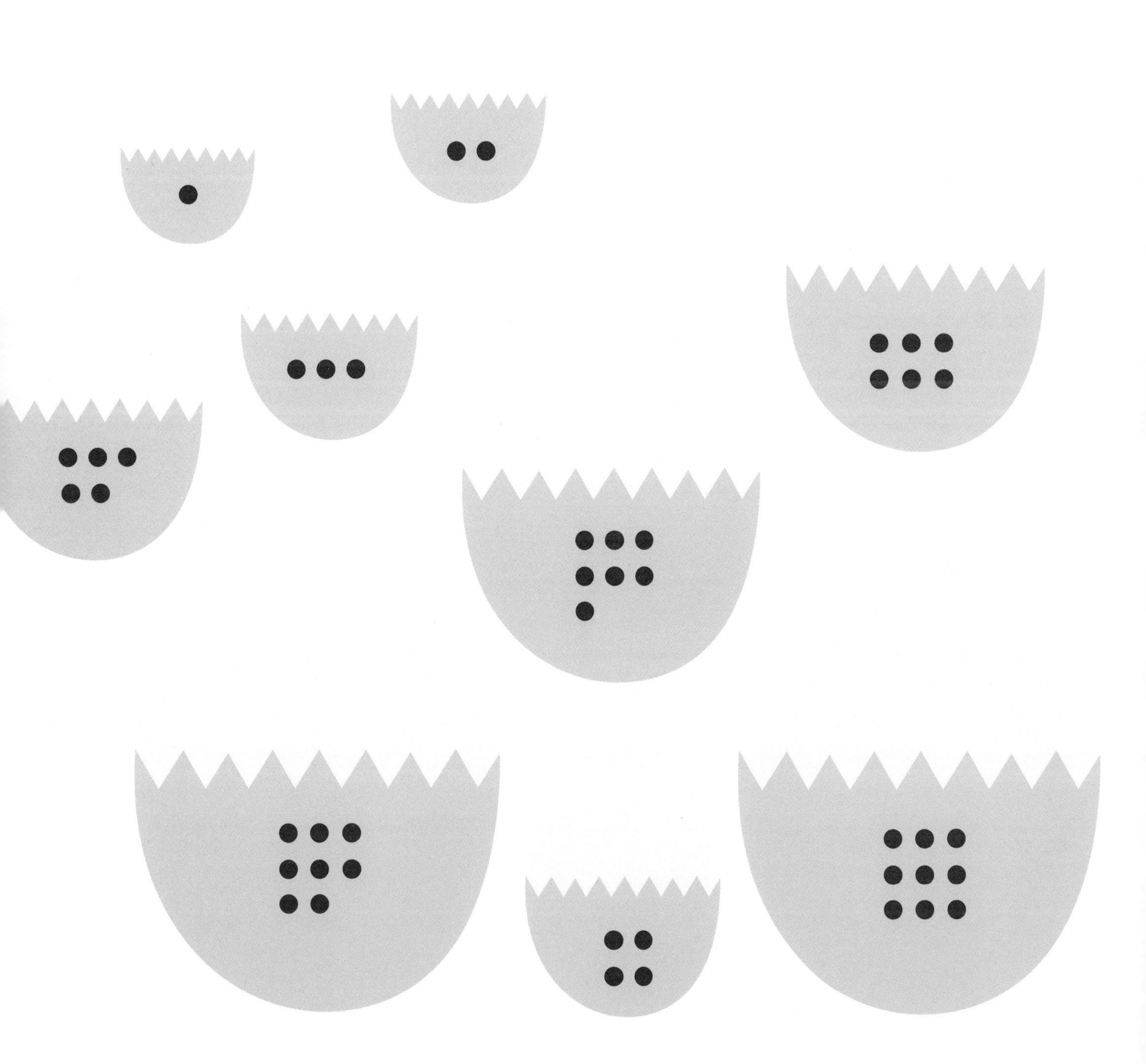

CUT OUT THESE NUMBERS ON THE DOTTED LINES.

IF YOU GLUE THE NUMBER TO A PIECE
OF CARDBOARD, YOU CAN KEEP IT AND USE
IT FOR NEW GAMES!

THEN CUT OUT THE LITTLE CARDS WITH
DIFFERENT NUMBERS OF FLOWER PETALS.
PRACTICE MATCHING THE NUMBERS
WITH THE CARDS THAT HAVE THAT
NUMBER OF PETALS.

ENJOY!

ONE, TWO, AND THREE

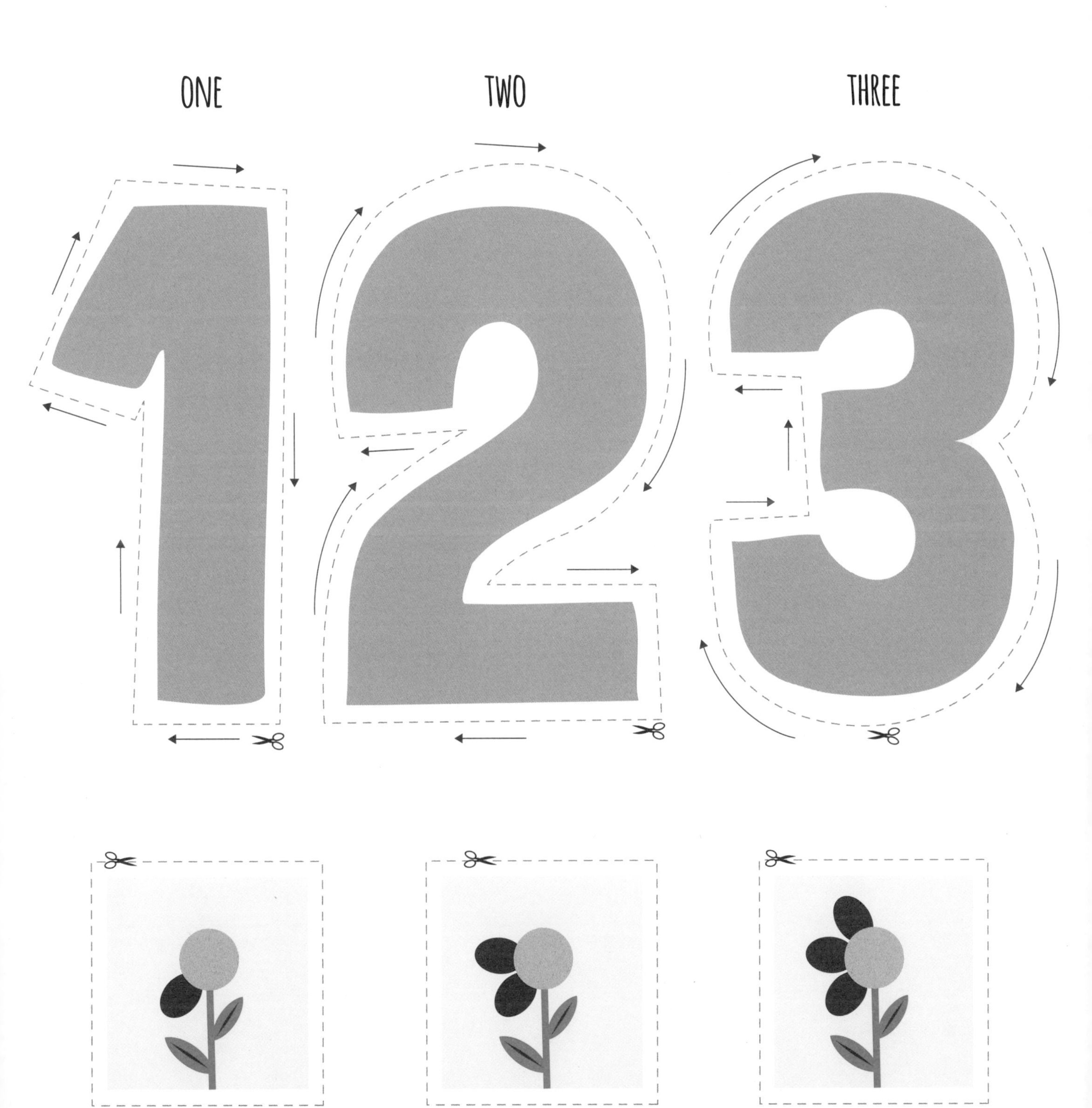

FOUR, FIVE, AND SIX

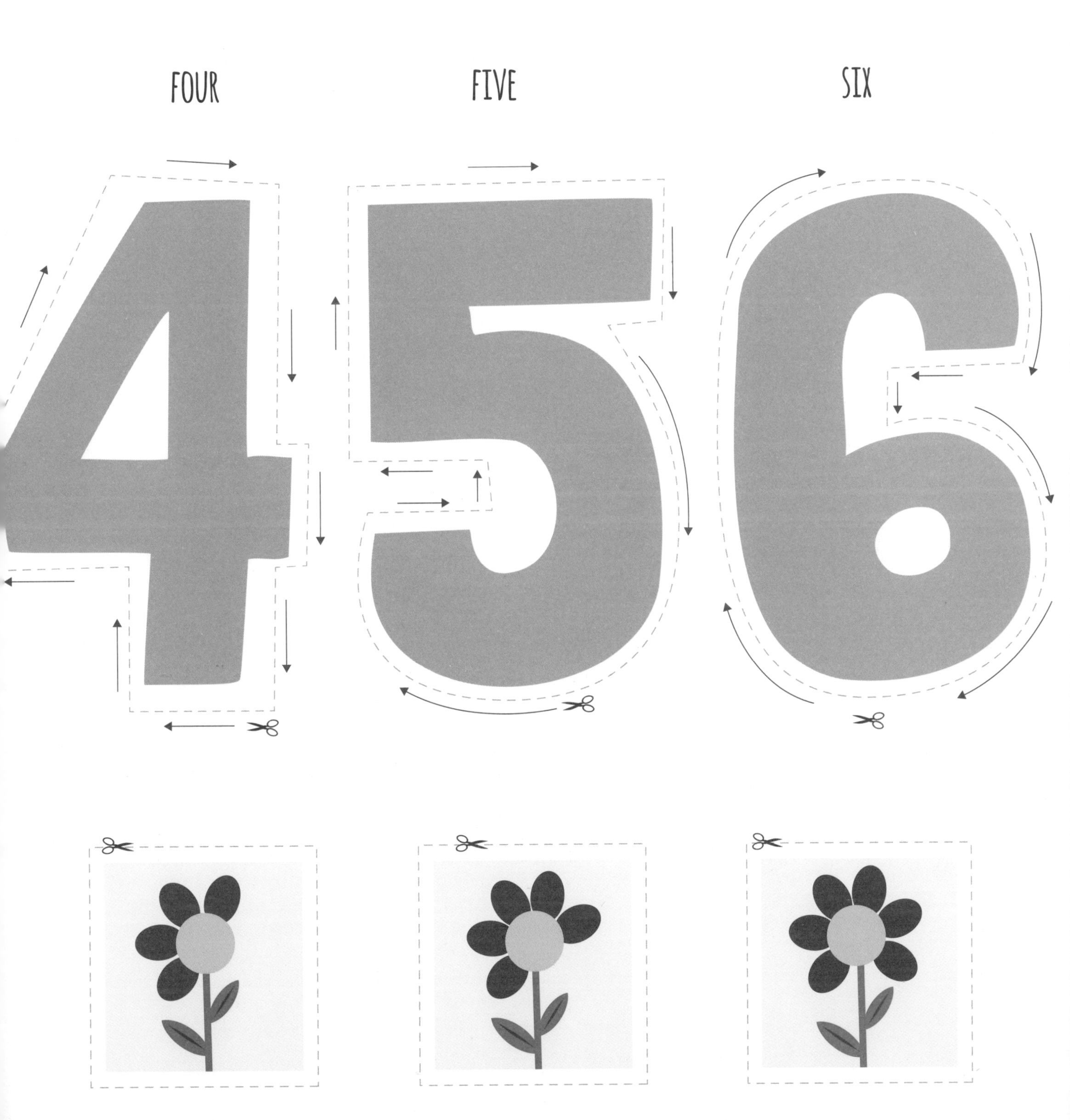

Seven, eight, and nine

WHAT TRAFFIC!

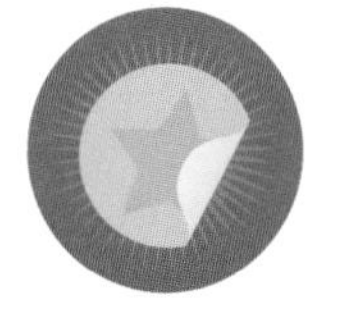
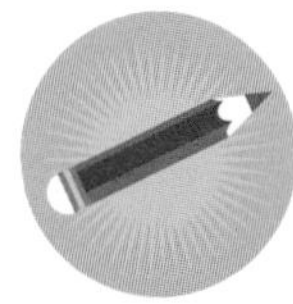

Find the stickers that go with WHAT TRAFFIC! at the back of the book.

Place the RED car stickers in the RED spaces and the BLUE car stickers in the BLUE spaces.

Count the red cars. Connect the dots from red to blue on the number you counted.

Then do the same thing with the blue cars.

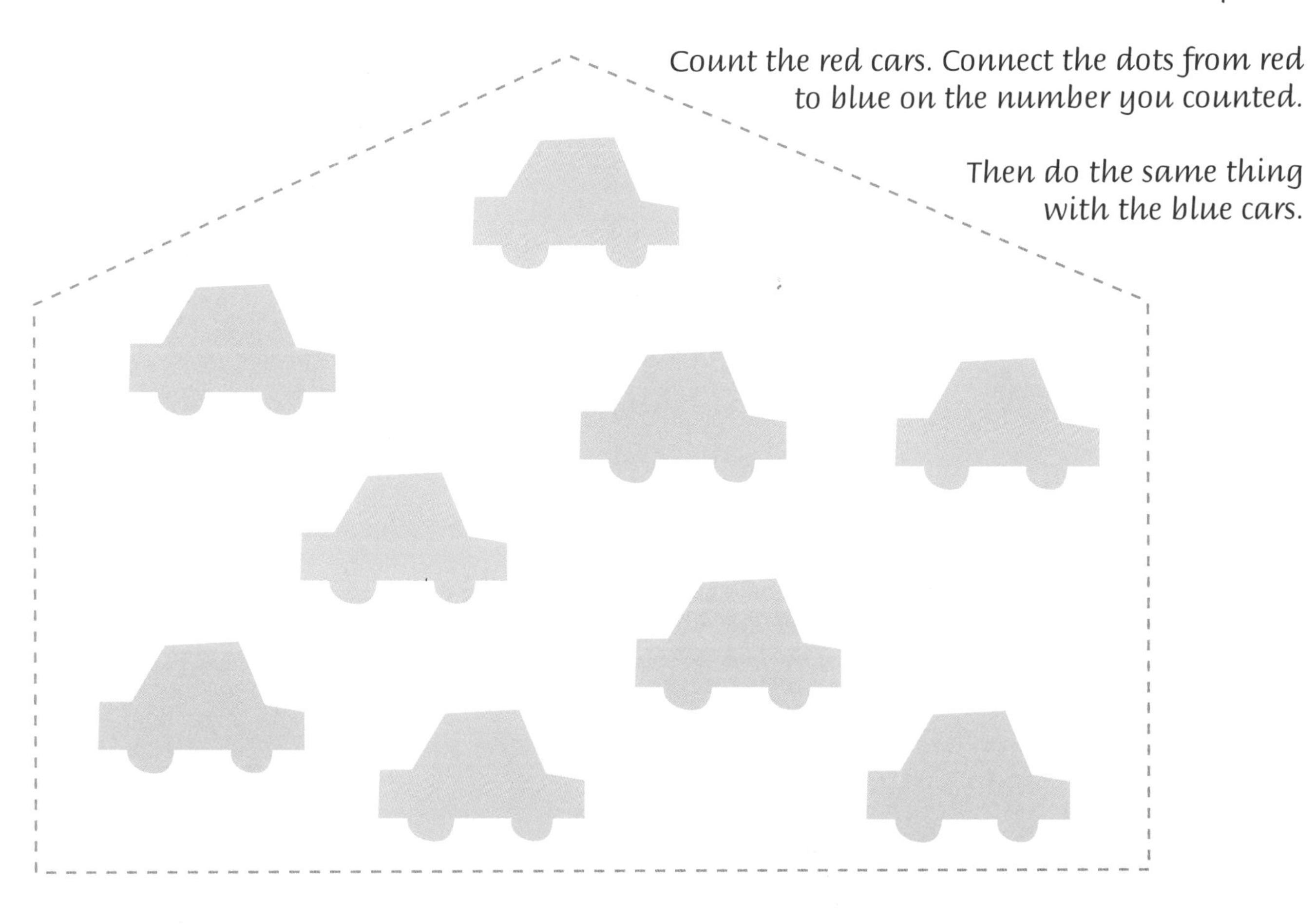

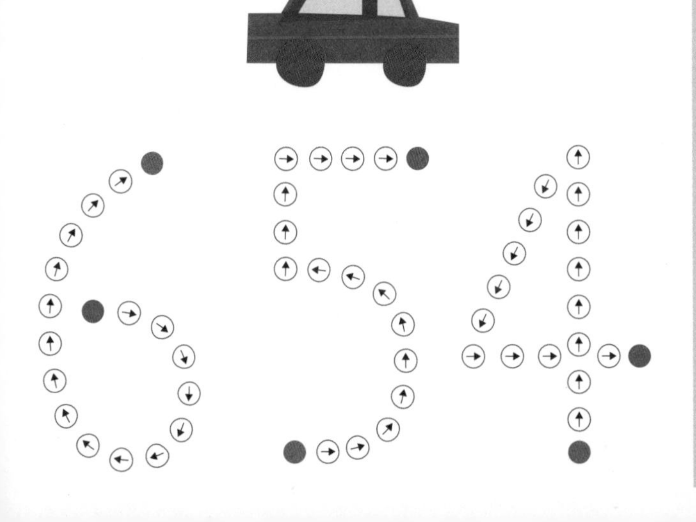
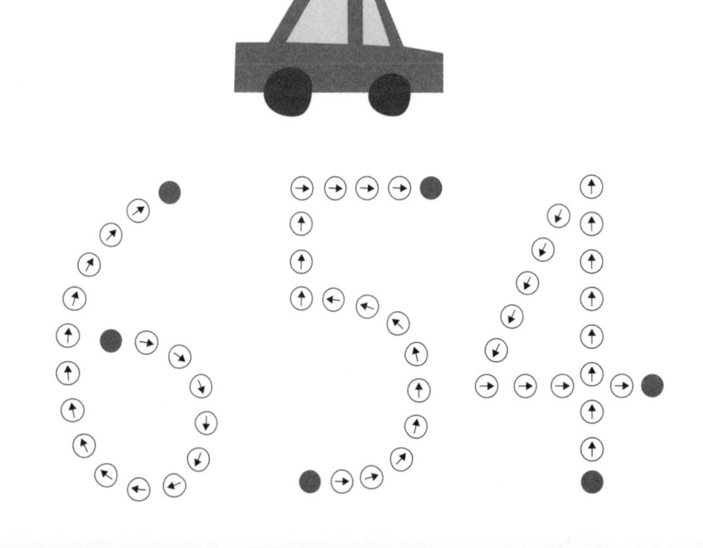

PEGGY'S VASES

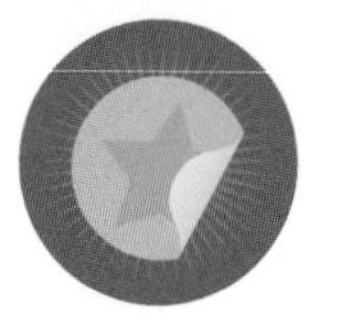

PEGGY IS FILLING HER VASES WITH FLOWERS, BUT SOME ARE STILL EMPTY!

Count the flowers in each vase.

Find the stickers that go with PEGGY'S VASES at the back of the book.

Choose the sticker with the number that corresponds to the quantity of flowers and stick it beneath the vase.

Color only the vases with ZERO flowers.

HOLD IT: HERE COMES ZERO!

Color the number.

Cut it out along the dotted lines starting from the red scissors.

Then cut out the little card and add the two to your matching game. Notice that the flower on the card has no petals--that's because zero means no quantity.

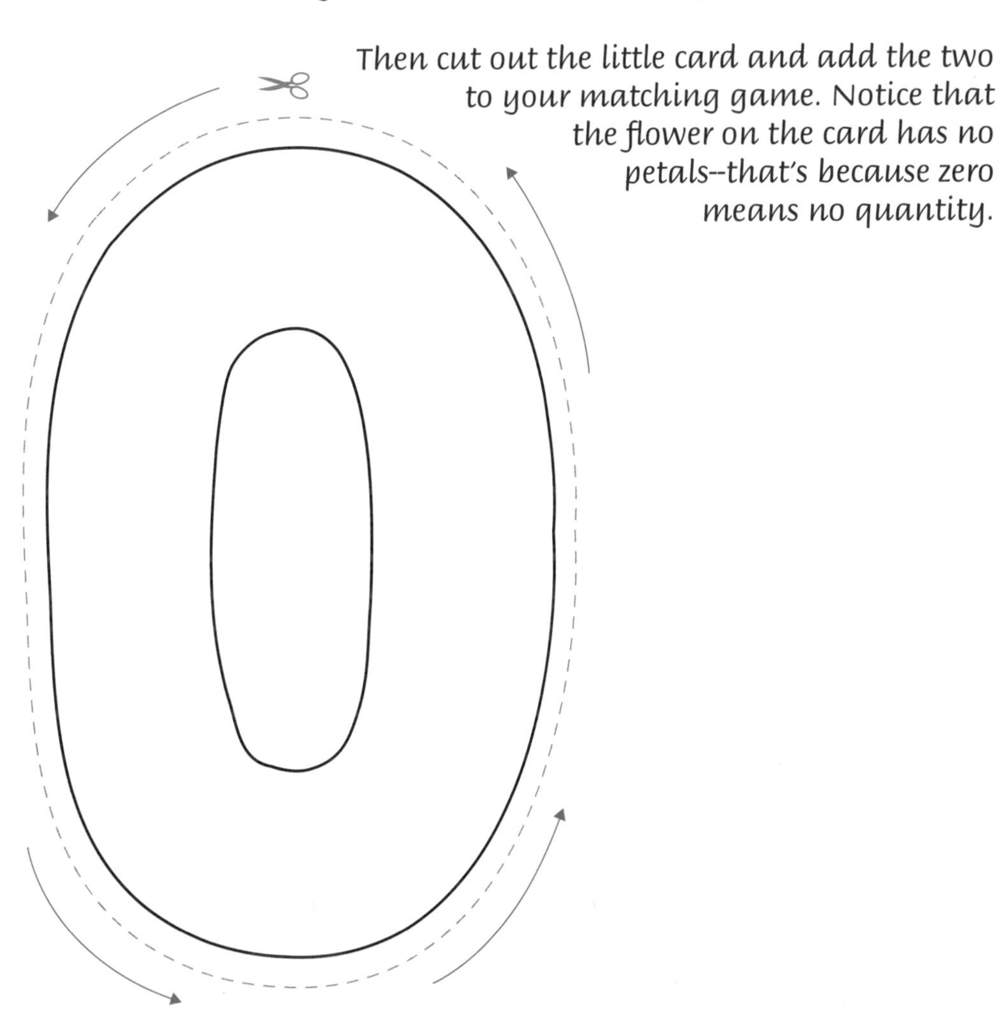

THE RABBITS' BALLOONS

THE FAIR IS HERE, AND LOTS OF LITTLE RABBITS HAVE BOUGHT BALLOONS. WHICH RABBITS HAVE NO BALLOONS?

Read the number next to each little rabbit.

Color as many balloons as are indicated by that number.

Then color the rabbits that have no balloons.

LET'S WRITE THE NUMBERS

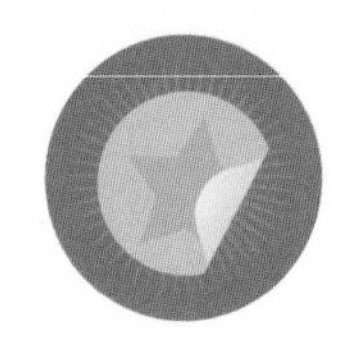

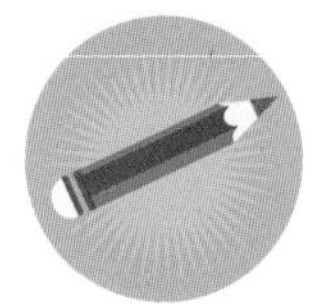

THIS LITTLE CRAB IS FAMOUS FOR MAKING PEARL NECKLACES.

HE IS MAKING SOME IN THE SHAPE OF NUMBERS.

Join the pearls, connecting the dots from the red ball to the blue ball.

Find the stickers that go with LET'S WRITE THE NUMBERS *at the back of the book.*

Look for the sticker that corresponds to each number and place it in the blank square near each number.

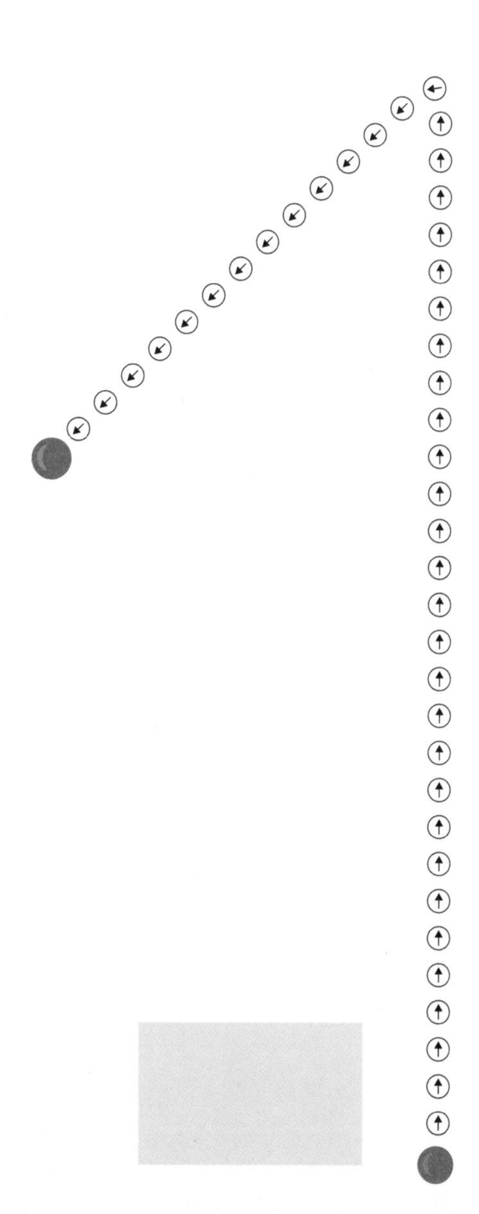

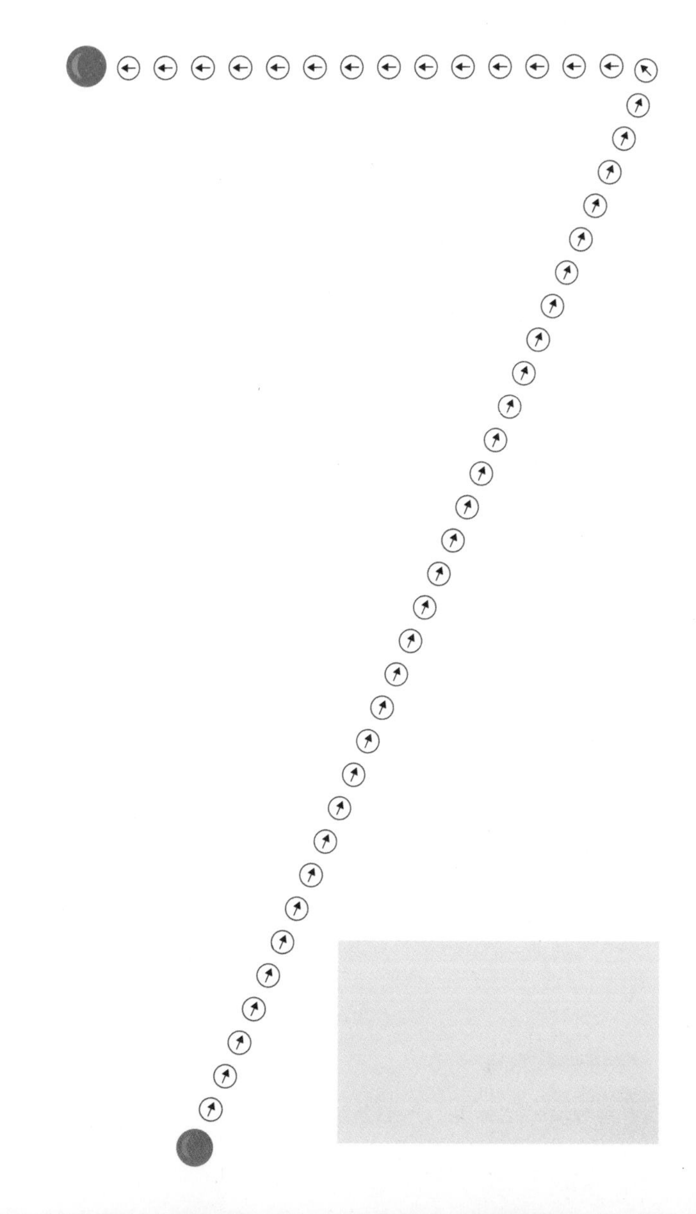

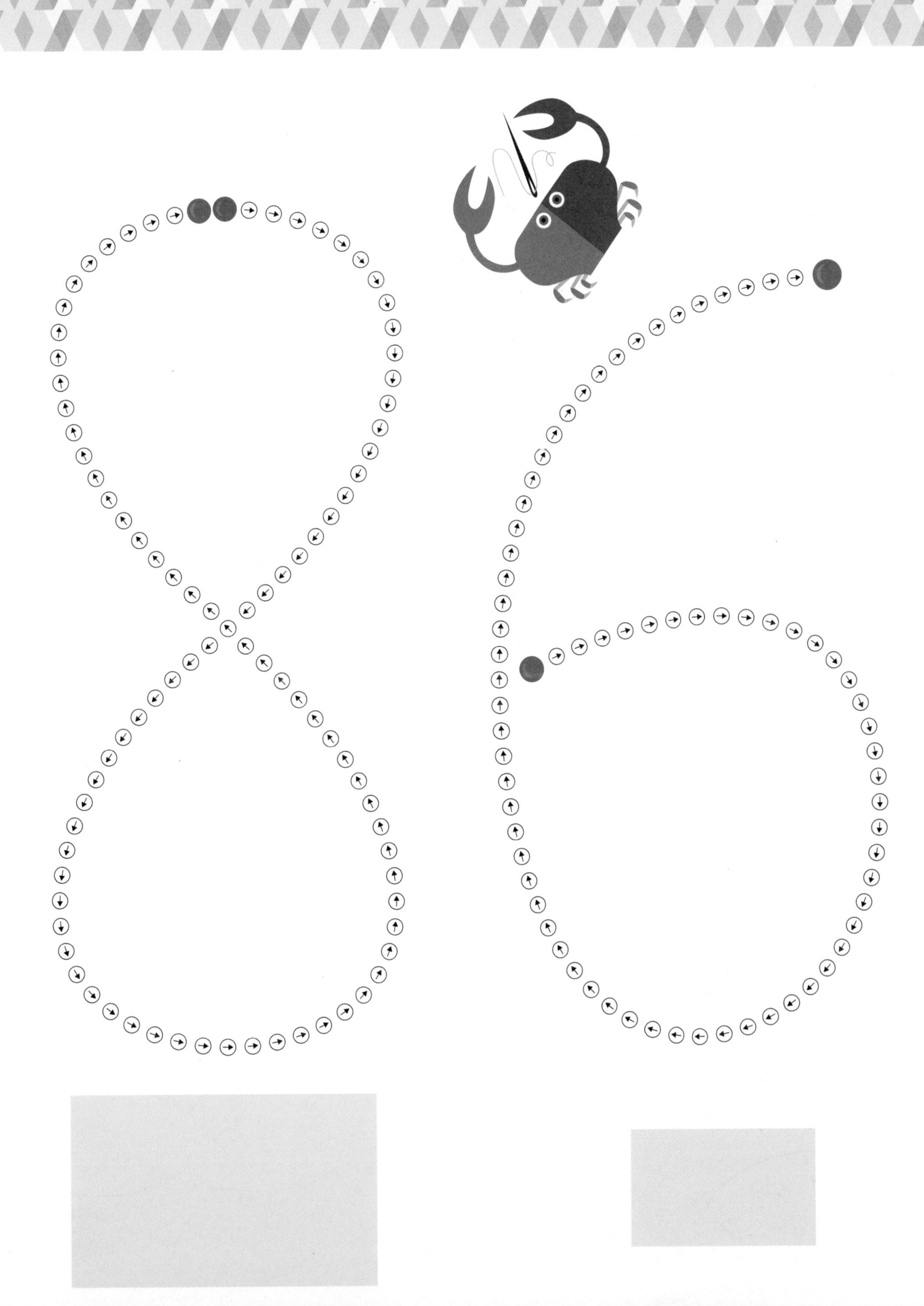

SO MANY STARS!

BEN IS VERY INTERESTED IN ASTRONOMY. OBSERVING THE PLANETS, HE HAS NOTICED THAT EACH OF THEM HAS A DIFFERENT NUMBER OF SATELLITES. COUNT THEM ALONG WITH HIM.

Count how many satellites each planet has.

Find the stickers that go with SO MANY STARS! *at the back of the book.*

Beneath each planet place the sticker for the corresponding number.

PROBLEMS IN LADYBUGLAND!

LADYBUGLAND HAS TWO BIG PROBLEMS: THE LADYBUGS HAVE LOST THEIR SPOTS AND THE PETALS OF THE FLOWERS ARE ALL TURNING GRAY! MAKE THINGS GO BACK TO THE WAY THEY SHOULD BE.

Say the number beneath each ladybug and in the center of each flower.

Draw that number of spots on each ladybug and color that number of petals on each flower.

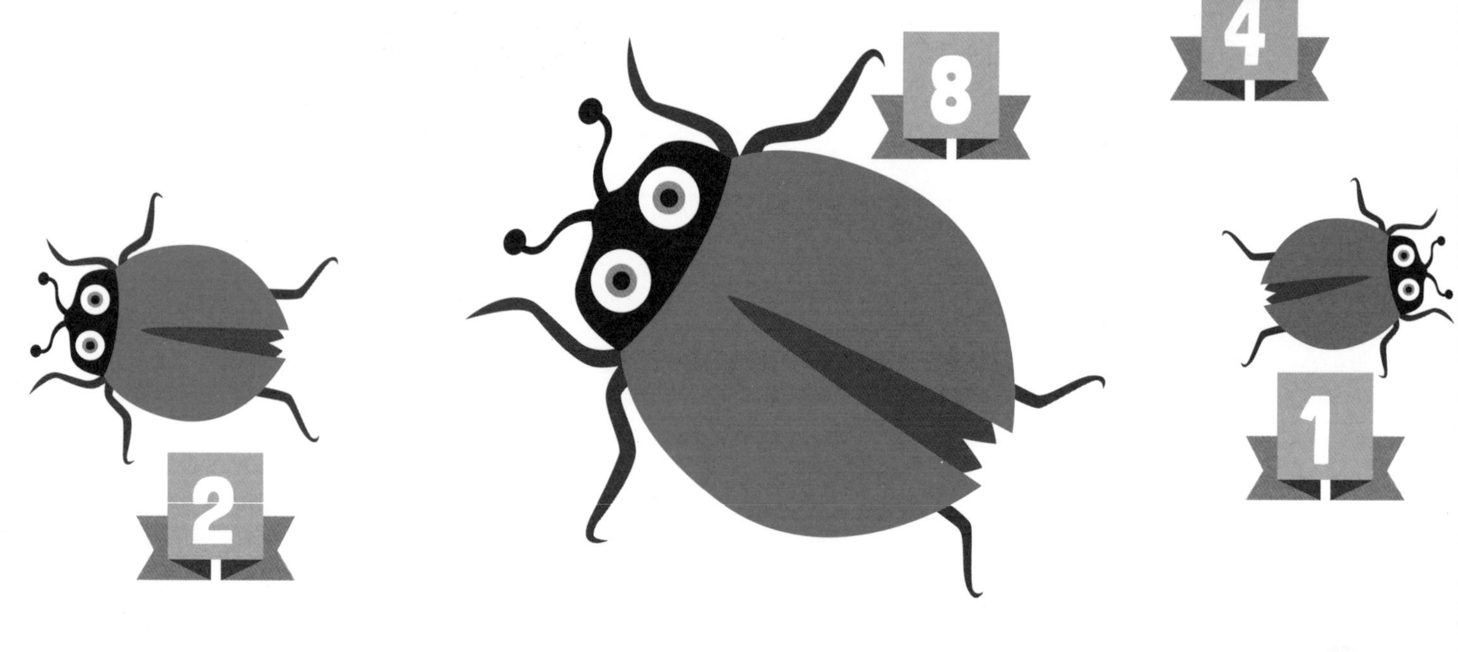

3
9
5
0
6
4
7
9
2

GRANDMA RABBIT'S SHOPPING

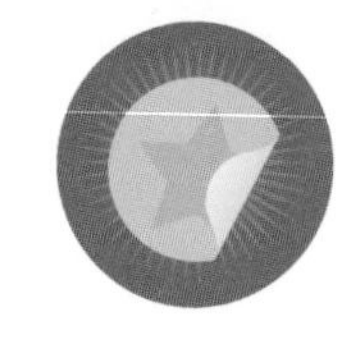

GRANDMA RABBIT IS VERY BUSY.
CAN YOU GO SHOPPING FOR HER?

Say the number beneath each basket.
Look for which fruit or vegetable to put in each basket.

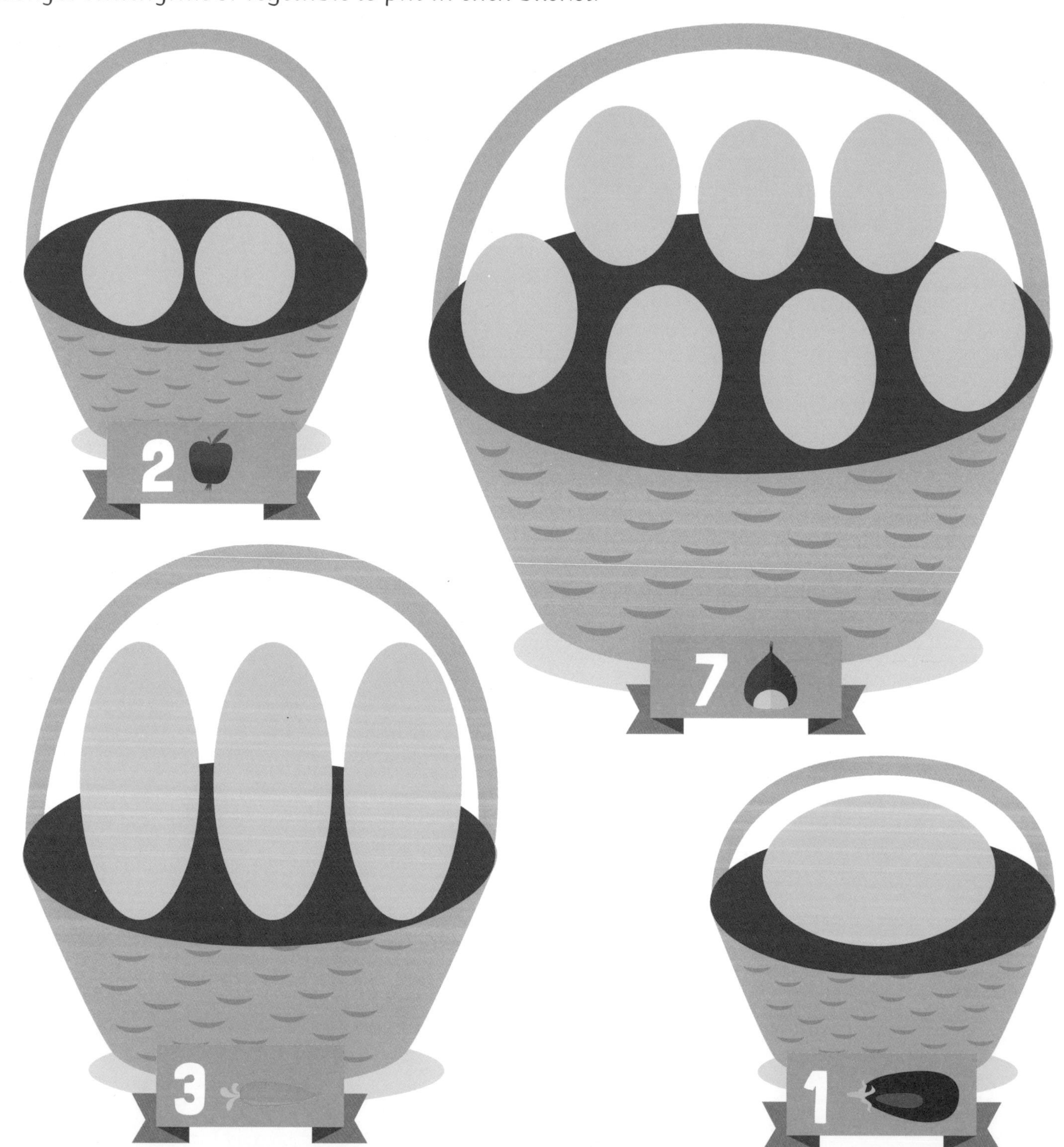

Find the stickers that go with GRANDMA RABBIT'S SHOPPING at the back of the book.

Place that number of stickers with that fruit or vegetable in each basket.

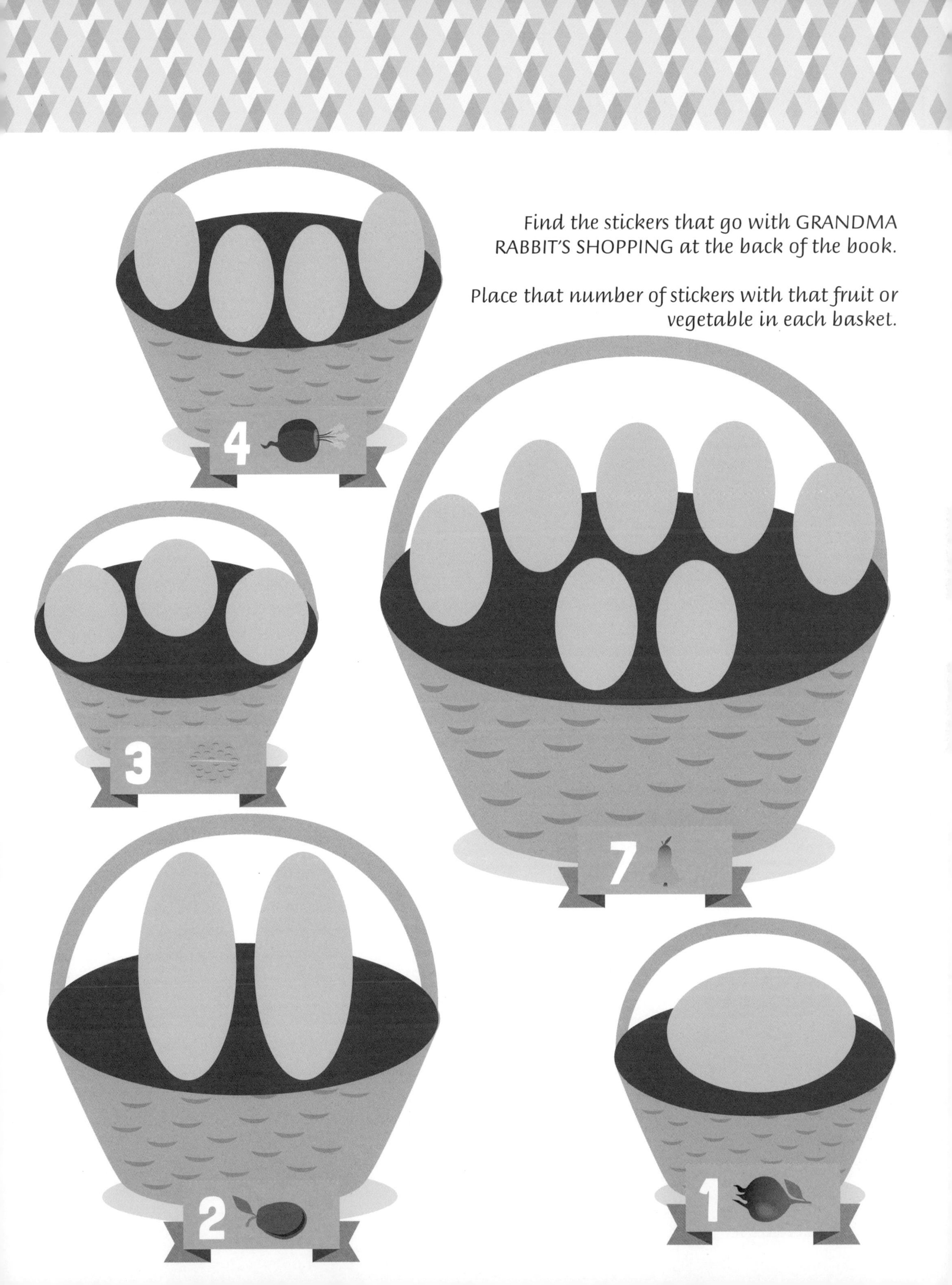

THE NUMBERS OF BENNY THE BEAVER

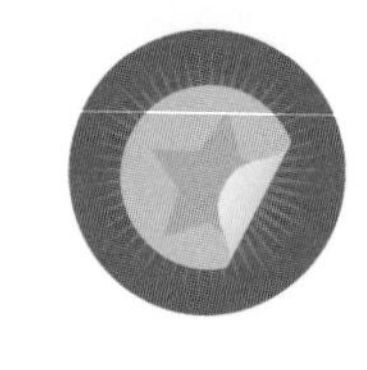

BENNY THE BEAVER HAS DESIGNED SOME PUZZLES FOR YOU TO SOLVE.

Find the stickers that go with THE NUMBERS OF BENNY THE BEAVER at the back of the book.

Look for the stickers that complete the shape in the lower picture.

Place the correct sticker in the correct space.

Say out loud the number you have built.

ZERO

TWO

ONE

THREE

FOUR
SIX
EIGHT
FIVE
SEVEN
NINE

THE LITTLE FISHES' BUBBLES

Count how many bubbles each fish makes.

Color the fish that make 4 bubbles YELLOW.

Color the fish that make 6 bubbles BLUE.

Color the fish that make 8 bubbles ORANGE.

THE SHOEMAKER OF ZOOLAND

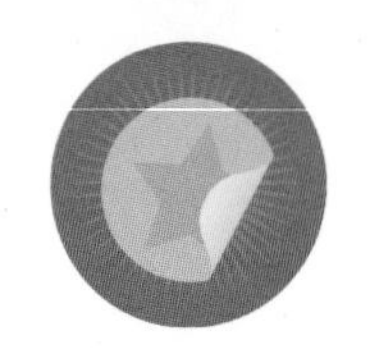

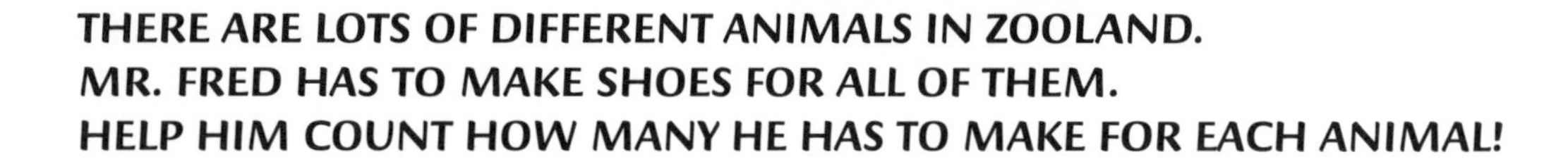

THERE ARE LOTS OF DIFFERENT ANIMALS IN ZOOLAND.
MR. FRED HAS TO MAKE SHOES FOR ALL OF THEM.
HELP HIM COUNT HOW MANY HE HAS TO MAKE FOR EACH ANIMAL!

Find the stickers that go with THE SHOEMAKER OF ZOOLAND at the back of the book.

Count each animal's paws.

Draw a circle around that number beneath each animal.

Then place that number of stickers on the paws of each animal.

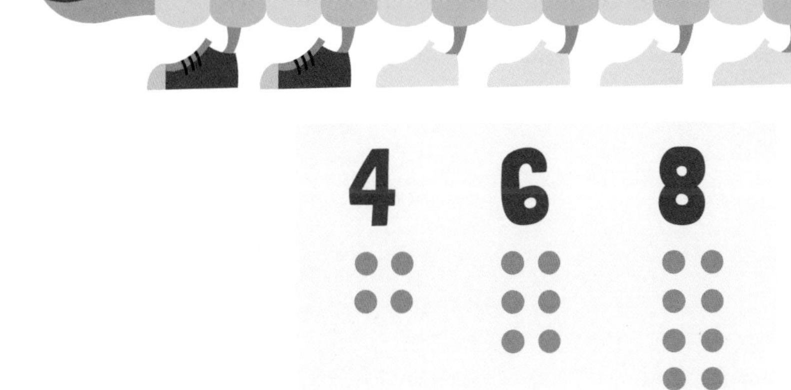

0 2 3

0 2 3

4 6 8

2 4 6

4 6 8

THE CARS OF THE TRAIN

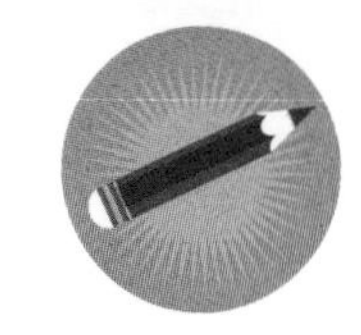
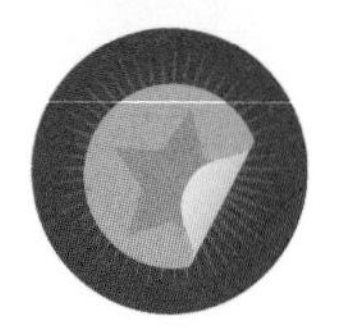

Find the stickers that go with THE CARS OF THE TRAIN
at the back of the book.

Place next to each train the stickers that correspond to the number of cars indicated.

Draw a circle around the longest train.

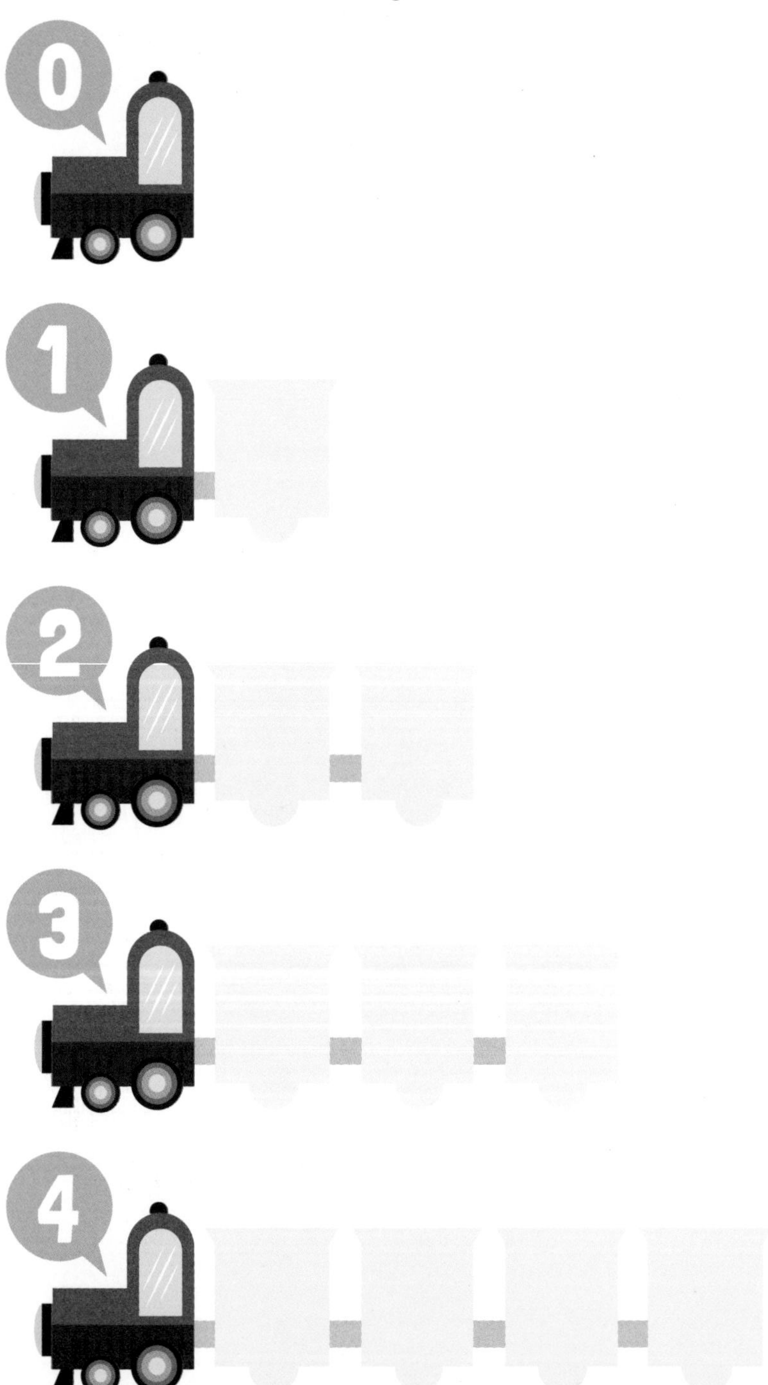

5
6
7
8
9

LIA'S LAUNDRY

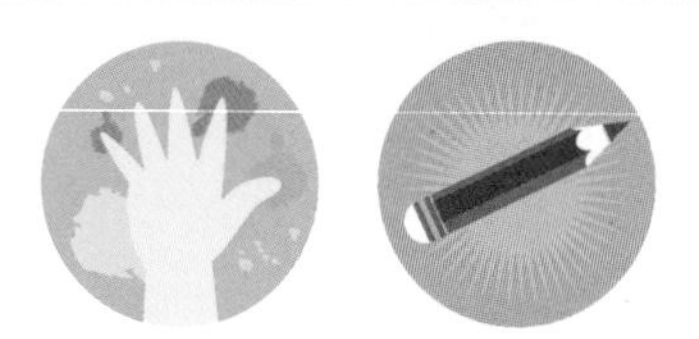

LITTLE LIA IS HELPING HER MOM BRING IN THE LAUNDRY. HELP HER PLACE IT IN THE RIGHT BASKETS.

Count how many striped shirts there are and color that number above the striped shirt basket.

Do the same thing for the other clothes, then draw a circle around the basket that contains the most clothes.

THE CHRISTMAS TREE

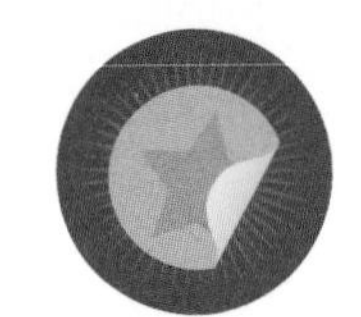

Find the stickers that go with THE CHRISTMAS TREE *at the back of the book.*

Use the number next to each ornament to decorate the tree!

Draw a circle around each decoration every time you attach a sticker to the tree.

1 

---

4    

---

5     

---

6      

---

7       

---

9 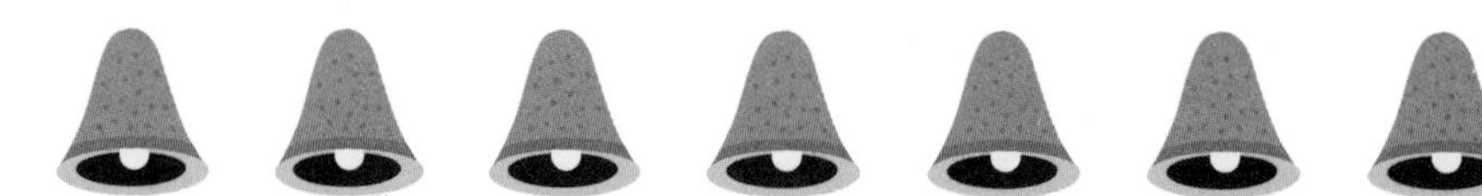        

THE JUMPING CONTEST

THE KANGAROOS HAVE ORGANIZED A JUMPING CONTEST! WHO WILL WIN?

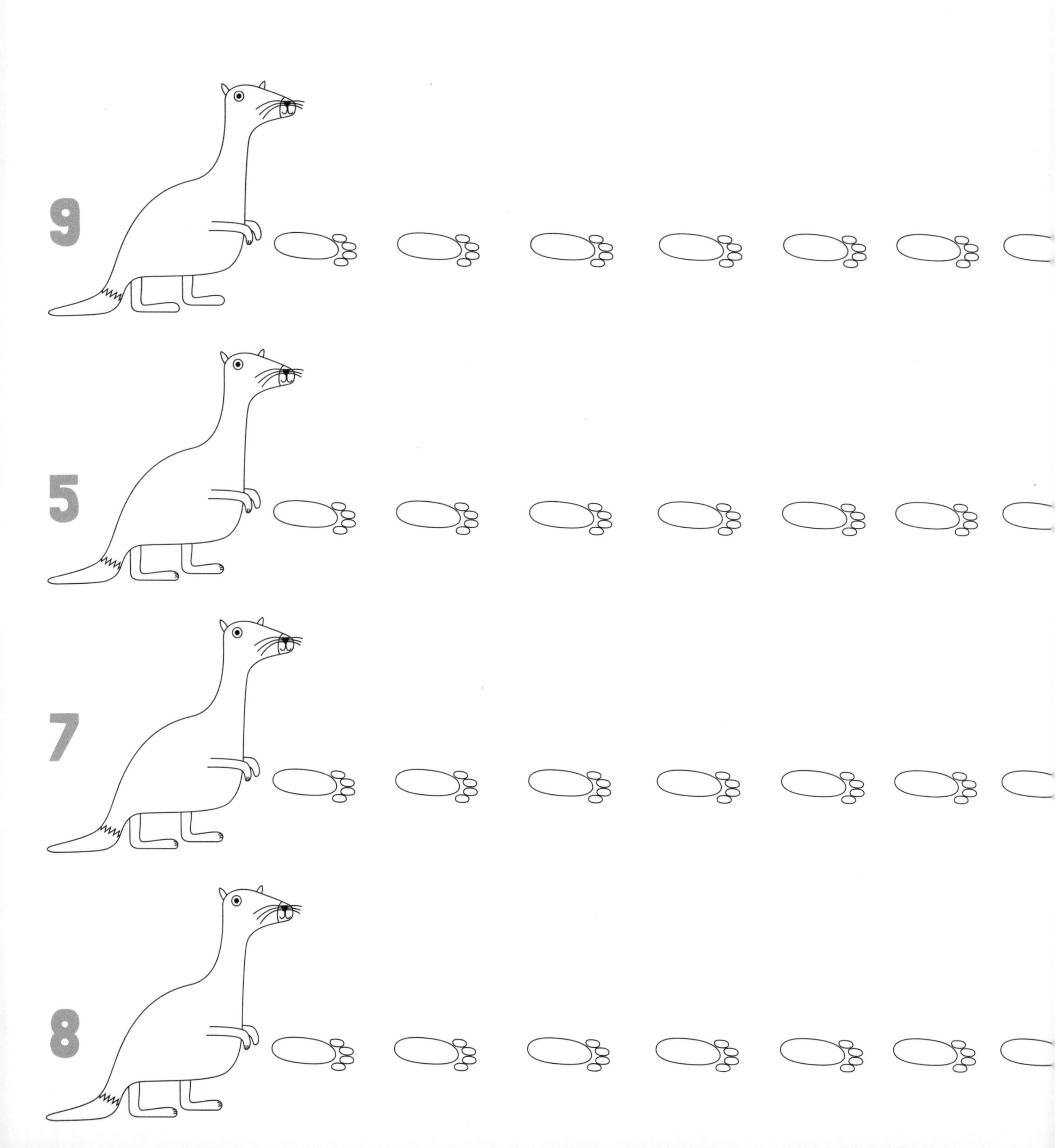

Color the number of footprints indicated by the number next to each kangaroo.

Who went the farthest? Color the kangaroo who made the most jumps and won the race!

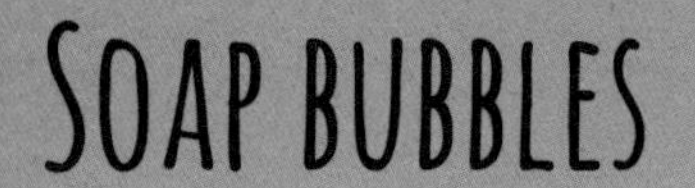

SOAP BUBBLES

**HOW MANY SOAP BUBBLES HAVE THE BABY ANIMALS MADE?
COUNT THEM BEFORE THEY BURST!**

Find the stickers that go with SOAP BUBBLES at the back of the book.

Count each baby animal's bubbles.

Place the sticker with that number in the squares next to each animal.

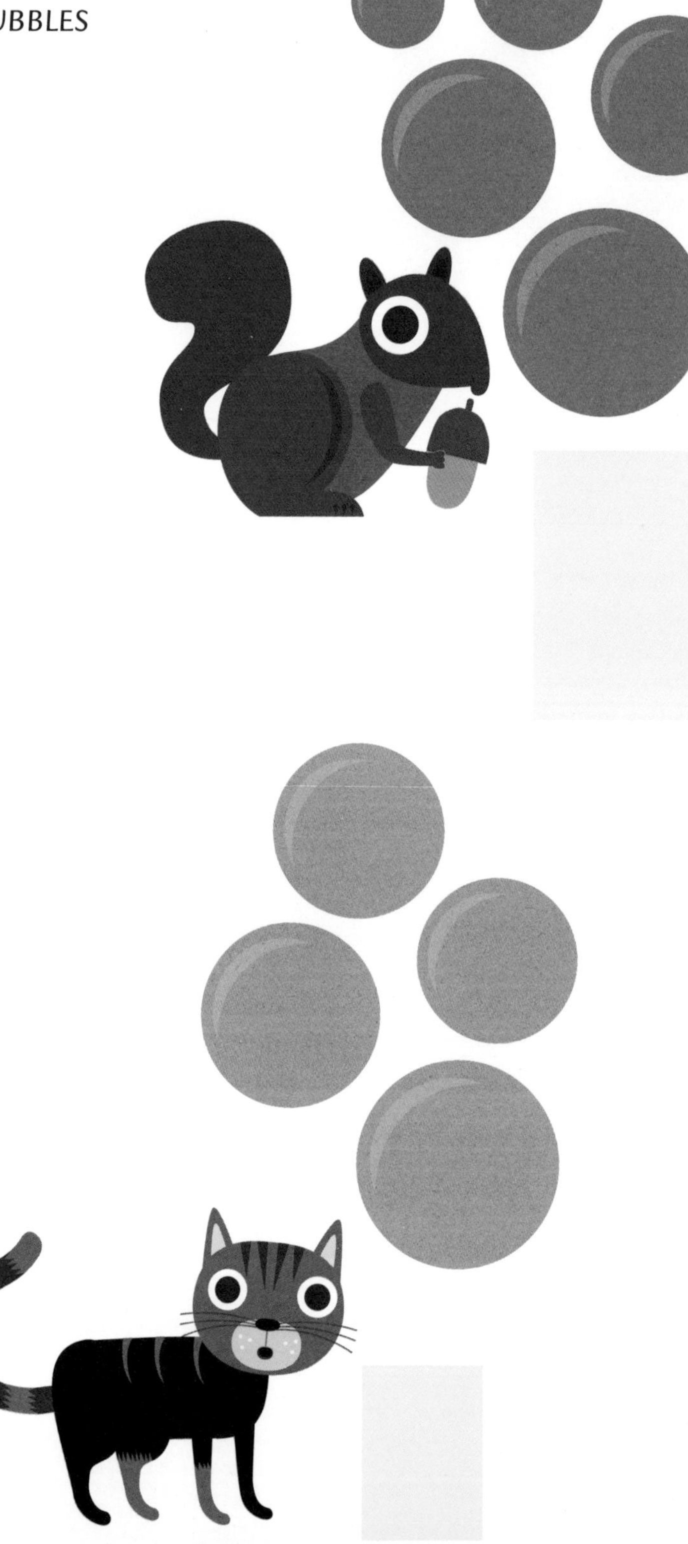

WHAT A LOVELY SMELL!

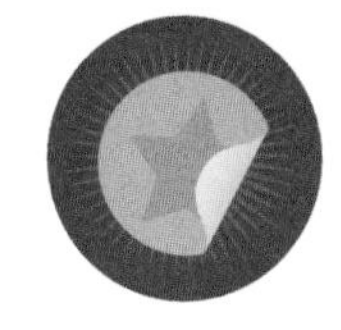

Find the stickers that go with WHAT A LOVELY SMELL! at the back of the book.

Place next to each ingredient as many stickers as are indicated by the number.

Now the cake can go into the oven. What a lovely smell!

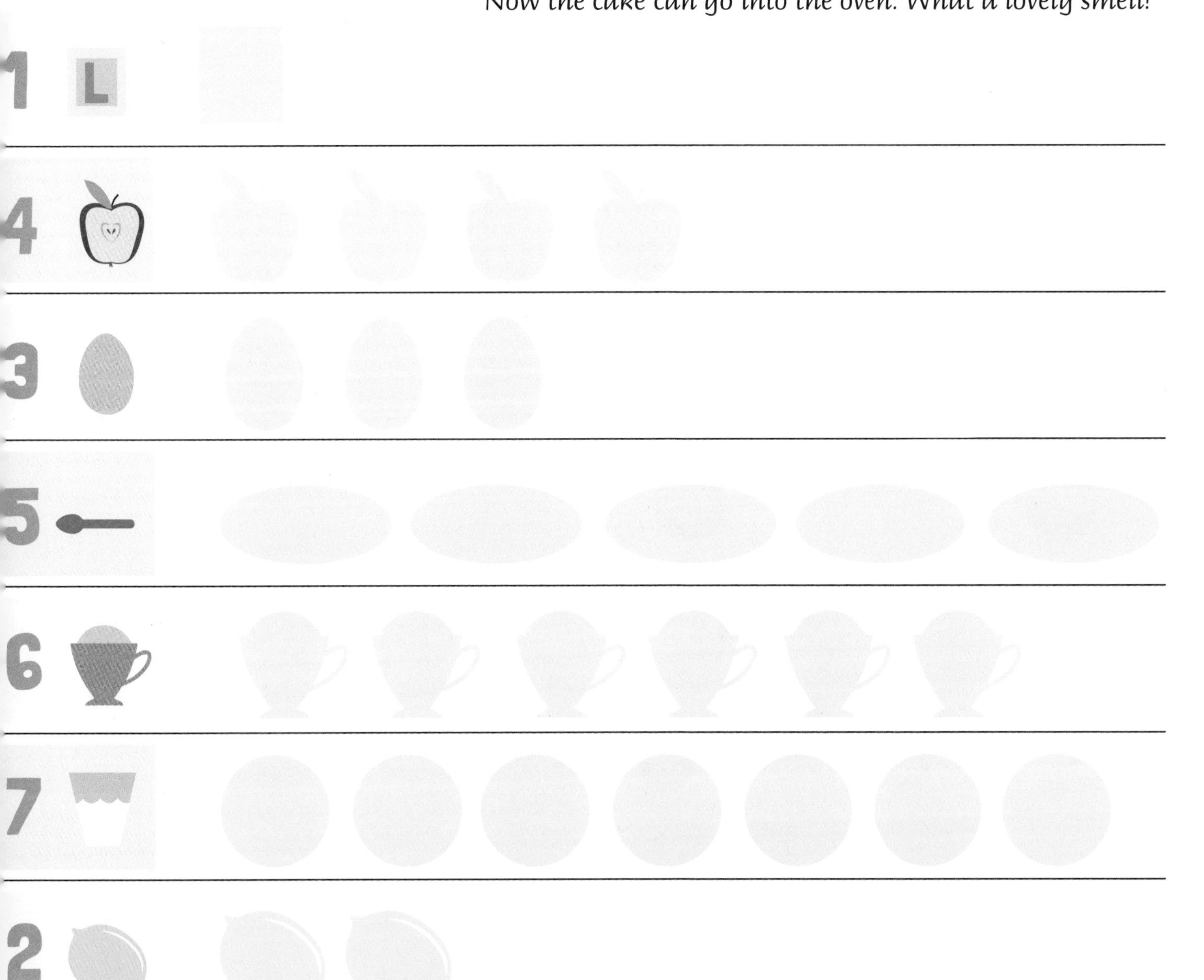

THE BABY ANIMALS GO ON A TRIP

**TODAY THE BABY ANIMALS ARE GOING ON A TRIP,
BUT THERE IS A GREAT DEAL OF CONFUSION!
HELP THEM GET ONTO THE RIGHT BUS:
CONNECT EACH GROUP OF BABY ANIMALS TO THE ONE BUS THAT CAN TAKE ALL OF THEM!**

Count how many baby animals
there are in each group.

Color the right number of baby animals.

Draw a line to link the group of baby animals
to the bus marked with the same number.

7

SKYSCRAPERS BEING BUILT

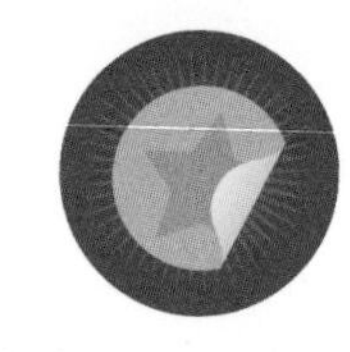
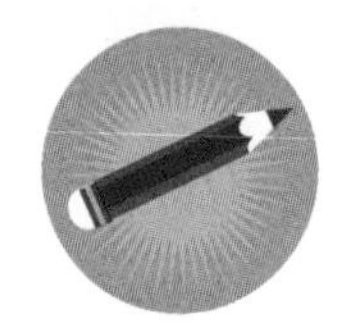

Complete the missing skyscrapers.

Find the stickers that go with SKYSCRAPERS BEING BUILT at the back of the book.

Place as many stickers on each building as there are floors missing.

Count the floors in the skyscrapers you have built.

Write the number of floors under each skyscraper.

... 1 ... 3 4

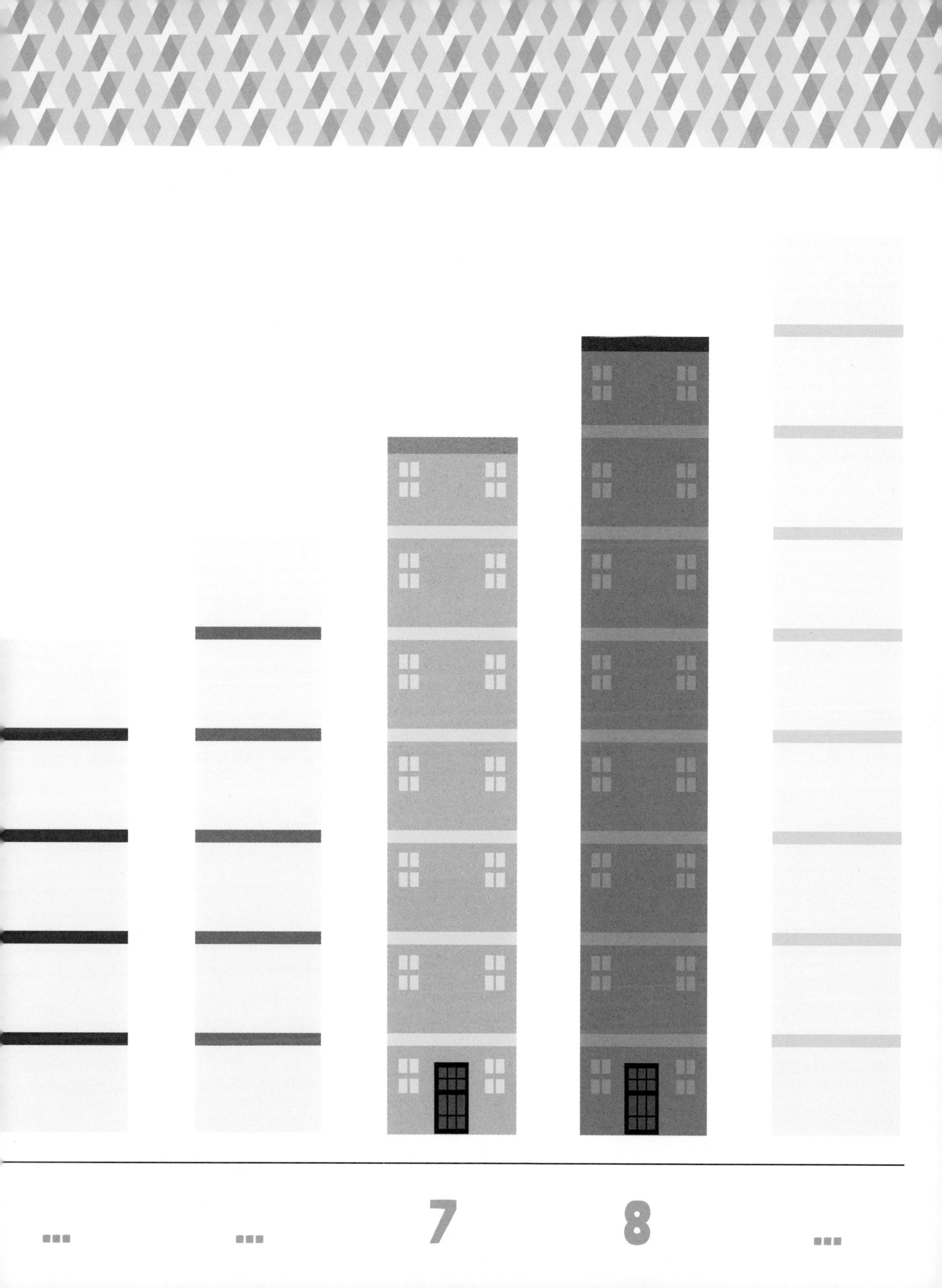

7
8

STERLING CHILDREN'S BOOKS
New York

An Imprint of Sterling Publishing
1166 Avenue of the Americas
New York, NY 10036

First Sterling edition published in 2018.

ISBN 978-1-4549-2847-8

Distributed in Canada by Sterling Publishing
c/o Canadian Manda Group, 664 Annette Street
Toronto, Ontario, Canada M6S 2C8

For information about custom editions, special sales, and premium and corporate purchases, please contact Sterling Special Sales at 800-805-5489 or specialsales@sterlingpublishing.com.

Manufactured in China
Lot #:
2 4 6 8 10 9 7 5 3 1
10/17

sterlingpublishing.com

Translation: Contextus s.r.l., Pavia, Italy
(translator: Martin Maguire)

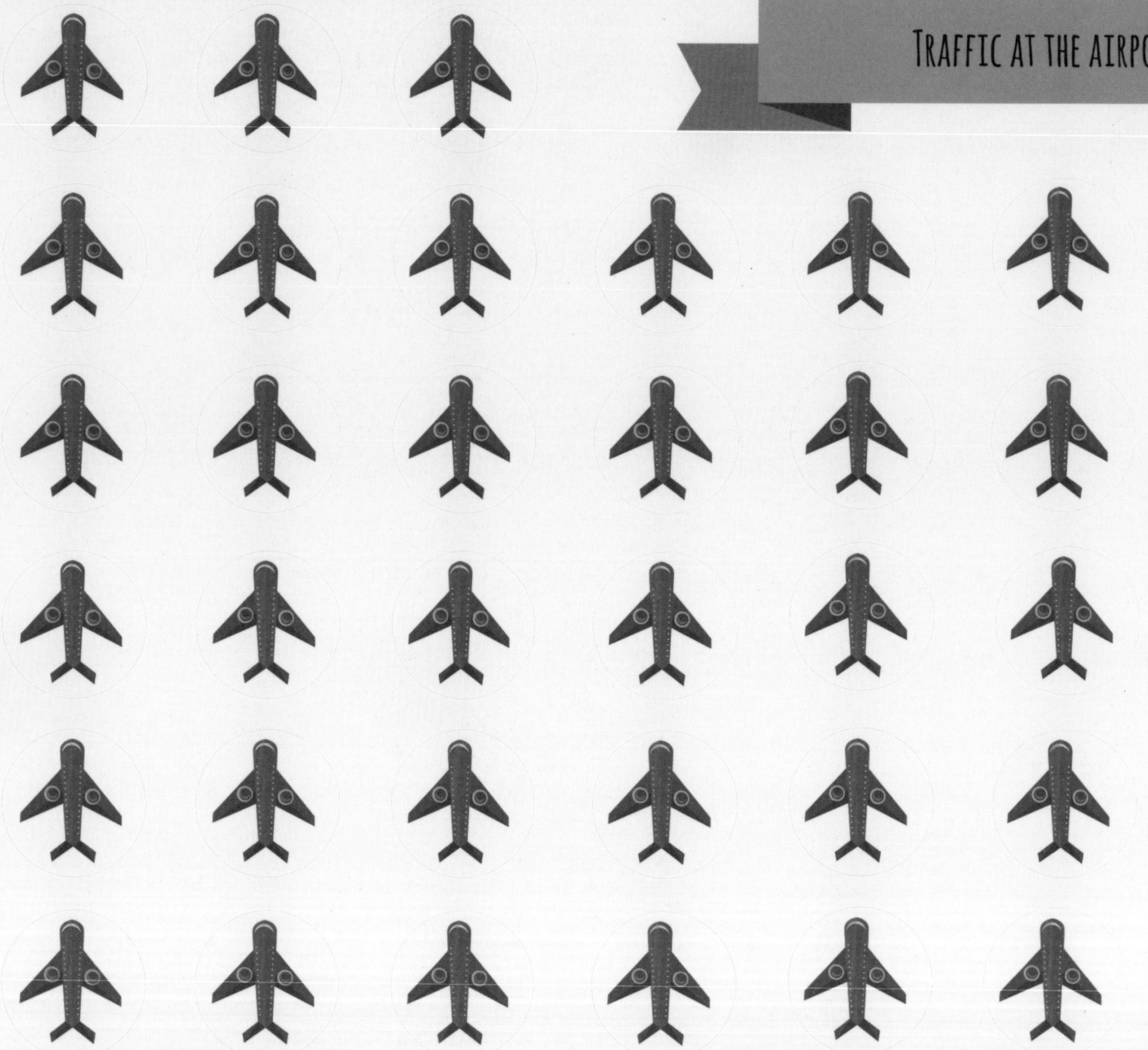

THE PETALS FLY AWAY

The ostrich eggs

1 2

3 4 5 6

7 8 9

What traffic!

Peggy's vases

1 4 5 6

1

LET'S WRITE THE NUMBERS

8 7 6

SO MANY STARS!

0 1 2 3 4 5 7

GRANDMA RABBIT'S SHOPPING

The numbers of Benny the beaver

The shoemaker of Zooland

The cars of the train

The Christmas tree

Soap bubbles

What a lovely smell!

7

5

4

L

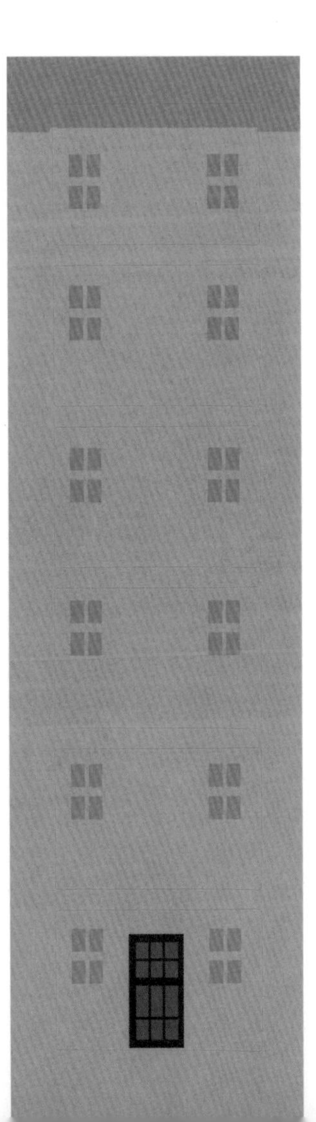

SKYSCRAPERS BEING BUILT